Where Are the Rocky Mountains?

by Sarah Fabiny

illustrated by Gregory Copeland

Penguin Workshop

For Milo—climb every mountain!—SF

For Shannon and Dave—GC

PENGUIN WORKSHOP
An imprint of Penguin Random House LLC
1745 Broadway, New York, NY 10019
penguinrandomhouse.com

Library of Congress Cataloging-in-Publication Data is available.

First published in the United States of America by Penguin Workshop, 2026

Manufactured in the United States of America
CJKW

ISBN 9780593890905 (paperback)
10 9 8 7 6 5 4 3 2 1

ISBN 9780593890912 (library binding)
10 9 8 7 6 5 4 3 2 1

The authorized representative in the EU for product safety and compliance is Penguin Random House Ireland, Morrison Chambers, 32 Nassau Street, Dublin D02 YH68, Ireland, https://eu-contact.penguin.ie.

Contents

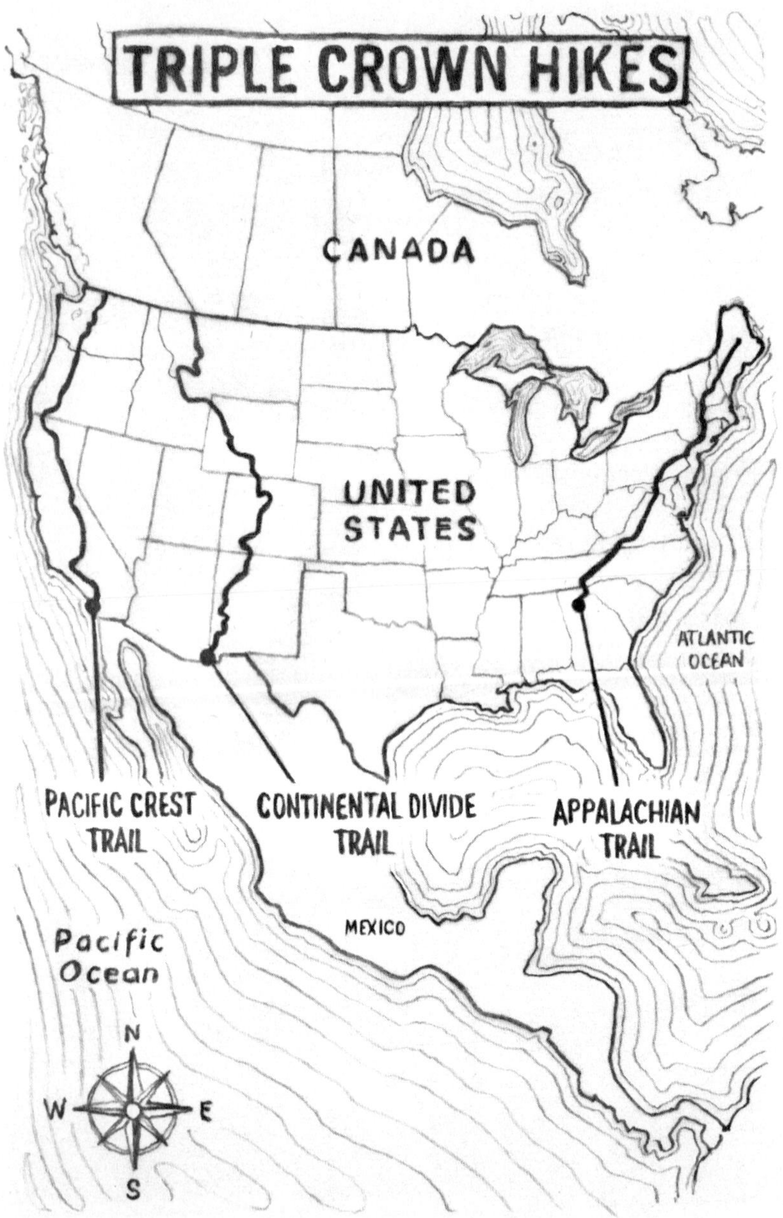
TRIPLE CROWN HIKES
CANADA
UNITED STATES
ATLANTIC OCEAN
PACIFIC CREST TRAIL
CONTINENTAL DIVIDE TRAIL
APPALACHIAN TRAIL
MEXICO
Pacific Ocean
N
W
E
S

Where Are the Rocky Mountains?

One of the most impressive accomplishments that a hiker can achieve in the United States is completing the Triple Crown, a challenging collection of incredibly long hikes. There are three hiking trails that come together to make the Triple Crown: the Appalachian Trail, the Pacific Crest Trail, and the Continental Divide Trail. The Appalachian Trail is more than 2,190 miles long and runs from Maine all the way down to Georgia. The Pacific Crest Trail winds through Washington, Oregon, and California, and is 2,653 miles long. The Continental Divide Trail (CDT) stretches about 3,100 miles through the Rocky Mountains from the border of Canada to the border of Mexico. Fewer than eight hundred people have managed to complete all three of these hikes, and the CDT is considered to be the most challenging. Fewer than half of all people who attempt to hike this trail actually complete it.

One of the reasons the CDT is so difficult to hike is because the entire route runs along the Rocky Mountains. The mountains have rocky, uneven trails and steep climbs that are challenging even for experienced hikers. The weather is also very unpredictable, with high winds and lightning frequently chasing travelers off the trail. It takes most hikers about six months to complete the hike. However, the trail passes through twenty-one wilderness areas, three national parks, and one national monument. So the three-thousand-plus miles are filled with some of the most stunning landscapes in North America—and the world.

If you decided to hike the CDT, you would cover only a fraction of the Rocky Mountains.

ALASKA
(US)
ROCKY MOUNTAINS
CANADA
PACIFIC
OCEAN
UNITED
STATES
N
W
E
S

The Rocky Mountains run up into Canada for one thousand more miles through the provinces of British Columbia and Alberta. (A province in Canada is similar to a state in the United States.) In fact, the Rocky Mountains are part of a collection of mountain ranges that run from Alaska all the way down to the tip of South America. This is why many call the Rocky Mountains the backbone of North America.

CHAPTER 1
Birth of a Mighty Mountain Range

The Rocky Mountains, also called the Rockies, are a natural wonder. They stretch more than three thousand miles, from Canada to New Mexico, and the peaks soar high into the sky. They rise up from the Great Plains, and many people travel from all over the world just to get a glimpse of them.

However, these mountains have actually come and gone several times. Forces of nature have built them up and worn them down over millions of years.

Around three hundred million years ago, during the Paleozoic Era, a mountain range called the Ancestral Rocky Mountains was being formed where today's Rocky Mountains now stand. (*Ancestral* means something from which another thing is descended.) The peaks of this earlier mountain range were not as high as the peaks of the Rockies we see today. Over millions of years, the forces of rain, rivers, and wind eroded these mighty mountains. They were reduced to sand and gravel. This sand and gravel became compacted and buried deep underground. Then, about seventy-five million years ago, the compacted sand and gravel, which makes up the modern Rockies, was pushed up by the forces of plate tectonics.

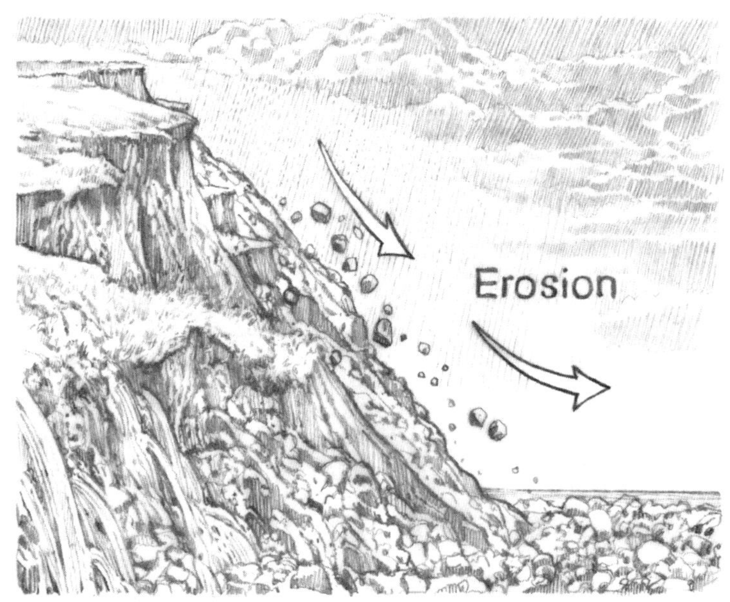

The outer layer of planet Earth is made up of slabs called tectonic plates. These plates cover very large areas and are about sixty miles thick. Although they are massive, the plates move. But they move very slowly, only around two to four inches a year. As the plates shift, their edges collide, drift apart, or slide past each other. Sometimes one plate will even slide underneath another plate. This is exactly what happened to create the Rocky Mountains we see today.

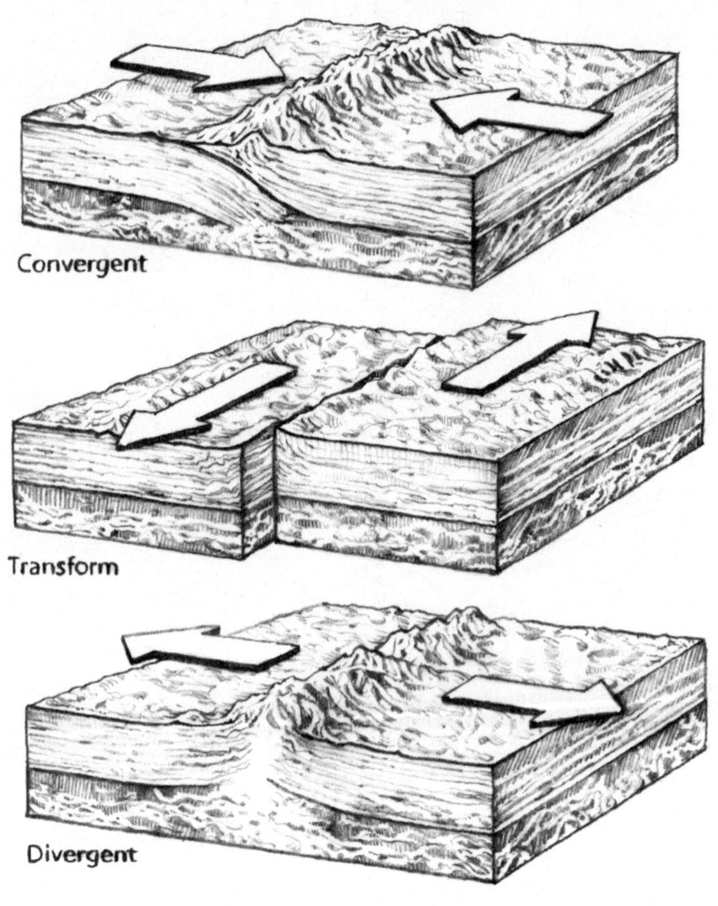

Types of tectonic plate movement. The Rocky Mountains were formed by convergent movement.

Hundreds of miles away from where the mountains now stand, a tectonic plate on the western edge of North America slid under another tectonic plate. As one plate dove down, the plate above it was pushed up. The plate underneath bulldozed its way hundreds of miles inland, and the plate above was uplifted into a series of folds, similar to wrinkles in a rug.

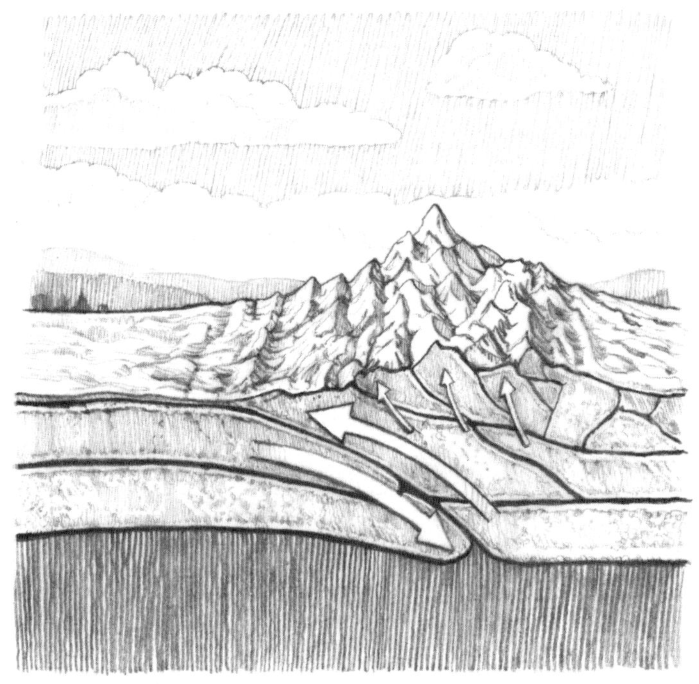

Over time, the forces of wind, rain, and rivers began shaping these mountains. Then, about ten million years ago, plate tectonics once again lifted up the entire region, by almost a mile. These are the peaks we see today.

The fact that it has taken millions of years to form the peaks of the Rocky Mountains might make you think that they are very old. However, the Rocky Mountains are much younger than other mountain ranges across the world. The Appalachian Mountains, which run along the eastern side of North America from Alabama up into Canada, are much older than the Rockies. They began forming 480 million years ago and were already wearing down by the time the Rocky Mountains started forming. That is why they have gentle, more rounded peaks. Time has worn down what used to be "spires"—which are sharp, pointed peaks—and mountaintops. But the Appalachian Mountains are babies themselves compared to other mountains around the world. The Black Hills in South Dakota are almost two *billion* years old! Found in South

Africa, the Barberton Mountains (also known as the Makhonjwa Mountains) are believed to be more than *three billion* years old!

Spires

Miles High

Because the young peaks and spires of the Rocky Mountains have not been around long enough to be worn down, they are pretty tall. The highest peak in the Canadian Rockies, Mount Robson in British Columbia, is 12,972 feet tall. The highest peak in the American Rockies is Mount Elbert in Colorado, at 14,438 feet tall. In Colorado

Mount Elbert

alone, there are fifty-four peaks that are over 14,000 feet high. That makes them over two and a half miles high—or as tall as ten Empire State Buildings stacked on top of each other! That's why Denver, Colorado, which is located in the Rocky Mountains, is known as the "Mile High City."

The mountains in Colorado that are over 14,000 feet tall are called fourteeners, and many climbers make it a goal to climb as many of these peaks as they can (or all of them). Albert Ellingwood is on record as being the first person to have climbed all of Colorado's fourteeners, which he did by 1925. However, Carl Blaurock and Bill Ervin claimed to have climbed Colorado's fourteeners by 1923. Mary Cronin is reported to be the first woman to have climbed all the fourteeners, which she did by 1934.

CHAPTER 2
From Snow to Sand

The Rocky Mountains stretch more than three thousand miles, but they aren't actually one continuous mountain range. The Rockies include at least one hundred separate ranges that are divided into four geographical zones: the Canadian and Northern Rockies, the Middle Rockies, the Southern Rockies, and the Colorado Plateau. A plateau is an area of raised land that is flat on top.

The Canadian and Northern Rockies include the mountains in Canada, Montana, and northern Idaho. The mountains in southern Idaho, Wyoming, and Utah are called the Middle Rockies. When people think of the Rocky Mountains, they tend to think of the landscapes

Colorado Plateau

of the Middle Rockies. This section contains the canyons, streams, waterfalls, and geysers found within Yellowstone National Park. The Southern Rockies run through Colorado and New Mexico. And the Colorado Plateau covers the Four Corners region of Utah, Colorado, New Mexico, and Arizona. It is called the Four Corners region because it is the only place in the United States where the borders of four states meet.

Mesa Verde

Mesa Verde, which means "green table" in Spanish, is one of the most well-known settlements built by ancient peoples. Located on the Colorado Plateau, it was a large complex of cliff dwellings established hundreds of years ago by ancestors of the Pueblo people.

Millions of years ago, flowing water carved out spaces in the sandstone of the canyon walls in the area. The settlers used these spaces to create their dwellings. The largest cliff dwelling has more than two hundred rooms and was home to as many as 250 people. The total population of Mesa Verde was probably around 5,000 people.

The area was hit with a drought in the late 1200s, and most of the settlers began to leave Mesa Verde. It is believed that they moved south, into what is now Arizona and New Mexico.

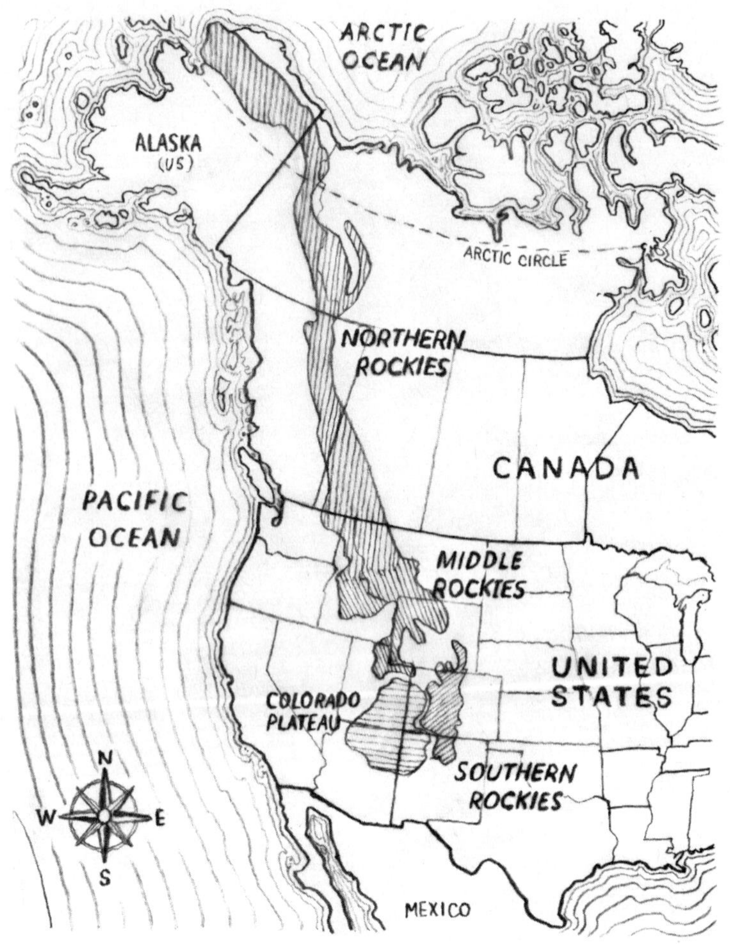

These four zones of the Rocky Mountains may be hundreds or even thousands of miles away from each other, but they do share some features: high elevations, shallow soil, lots of minerals, and stunning scenery. However, they are quite different in the types and ages of the rock that makes up the many mountains, the physical features of each area, and the climates of the four zones. If you decided to walk the Continental Divide Trail from Canada to Mexico, you would see everything from thick pine forests and snow-covered peaks in the Canadian and Northern Rockies to prickly cactuses and dry desert in the Southern Rockies. You would also see areas with rolling foothills surrounding the high mountain peaks, and areas where the mountains suddenly and sharply rise up from flat plateaus. The Rocky Mountains provide a diverse and wide range of landscapes and environments.

The Columbia Icefield

The Columbia Icefield is located in the Canadian Rockies along the border of the Canadian provinces of British Columbia and Alberta. An ice field is a large, flat mass of ice. The Columbia Icefield is about seventeen miles long, up to 1,200 feet deep,

and covers around a hundred square miles. It receives about twenty-three feet of snow each year. Not all of that snow melts during the short summers, so it often builds up. The compacted snow turns to ice, which flows outward through the surrounding mountain passes. This creates areas of ice known as glaciers. The ice field feeds into six major glaciers, including the Athabasca Glacier, which is the biggest of the six.

Because of harsh weather conditions and its isolated location, the Columbia Icefield was one of the last major geological features in western Canada to be visited and recorded by Europeans. Today, however, it is a popular tourist destination.

Not only are the Rocky Mountains split into four geographical zones, they are also divided into different ecological zones. An ecological zone is an area that has certain characteristics that set it apart from surrounding areas. The characteristics that set zones apart are climate, the types of plants and animals that live in the zone, and, most importantly, elevation. The Rockies can be divided into six zones: plains, foothills, lower montane, upper montane, subalpine, and alpine.

The plains are a flat, grassy area. They are most often found at the base of the mountains or in valleys between mountains.

The foothills are where the plains begin to change into steeper mountains. It is an important ecosystem that provides homes for many plants and animals. Foothills can range in elevation from a few hundred to several thousand feet.

Plains

The lower montane zone is found on lower mountain slopes. It is a generally cool, moist area filled with deciduous and coniferous trees.

(Deciduous trees have leaves that change color and fall off. Coniferous trees are evergreens that have needle-shaped leaves.)

Lower montane zone

The upper montane zone is found on upper mountain slopes. It is cooler and wetter than the lower montane zone. The trees found here are mostly coniferous trees. Together, the lower and upper montane zones are found between 5,600 and 9,500 feet.

Upper montane zone

Subalpine zone

The subalpine zone is located just below the tree line. (The tree line is the point on a mountain above which trees can't grow.) This zone usually has strong winds and harsh, cold temperatures.

Alpine zone

Finally, the alpine zone is located above the tree line. It has rocky cliffs, snowfields, glaciers, and very harsh conditions. The sharp, snowy mountain peaks, at heights of 12,000 to more than 14,000 feet, are in this zone.

East or West?

The mighty Rocky Mountains aren't just the backbone of the North American continent. They also determine which way rivers flow. The Rocky Mountains create the continental, or great, divide in North America. A continental divide is a ridge or boundary that separates a continent's river systems. Each river system flows into a different body of water. In general, rain or snow that falls on one side of the divide flows one way, and rain or snow that falls on the other side flows in the opposite direction. In the Rocky Mountains, on the eastern side of the divide, all water flows toward the Gulf of Mexico and the Atlantic Ocean. On the western side, all water flows toward the Pacific Ocean.

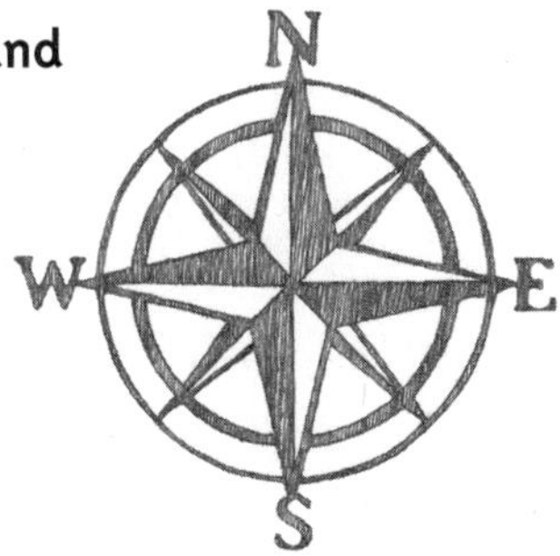

CHAPTER 3
The First Peoples of the Rocky Mountains

The Rocky Mountains were formed millions of years ago, and the first people on Earth who look like us are thought to have been living in Africa about 130,000 years ago. However, the first people living in the Rocky Mountain region didn't arrive there until after the most recent ice age, which ended around 13,000 to 14,000 years ago. These people are often referred to as Paleo-Indians.

Some scientists believe that these first settlers arrived on the North American continent by traveling over a formation called the Bering Land Bridge that connected Asia and North America. This land bridge is now covered by the Bering Sea,

Paleo-Indians

but it was dry land back then. Some people believe that humans traveled across the bridge to live in North America. However, most indigenous tribes of the Rocky Mountains believe that their ancestors first appeared in North America and did not migrate across the Bering Land Bridge.

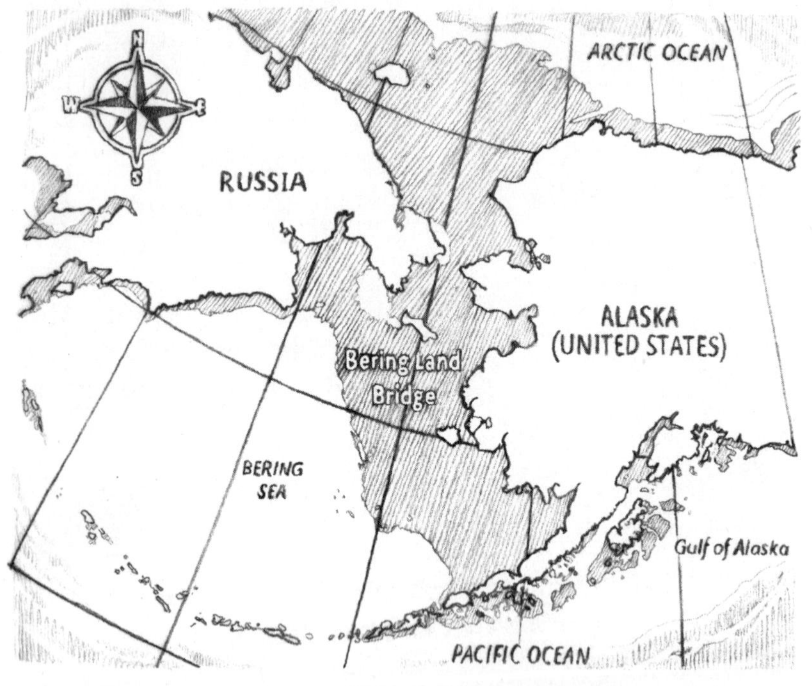

Over time, the climate became warmer and drier, so the continent became home to all kinds of plants and animals. And as the number of animals and plants increased, so did the number of people who lived there. These humans hunted, fished, and gathered plants.

The animals that these first settlers hunted included now-extinct species, such as mastodons, giant ground sloths, and giant beavers. (A species is a group of living things that are all very much alike and are descended from the same ancestors.)

Mastodon

The settlers also hunted the ancestors of the bison that we see today.

Archaeologists have discovered spear points that the first settlers used to hunt and kill large prehistoric creatures. (An archaeologist is someone who studies the things that people made, used, and left behind in ancient times.) Archaeologists have also found stone knives and scraping tools that the Paleo-Indians used to cut up the creatures they killed and scrape their hides. The hides were used for clothing and shelter.

These first people to come to North America traveled from one area to another in search of food and water but never settled in one permanent location. They probably moved their camps several times a year depending on the season. They tracked animals as they made their way through the mountains, moving to the lower foothills and plains in the fall and winter and into the mountains during spring and summer.

The trails that these prehistoric animals and ancient people used can still be seen in the Rocky Mountains today, and some modern roads still follow their paths.

Over the next few thousand years, the climate changed. It varied from warm and dry to cool and wet. The plants and animals living in the Rocky Mountains had to adapt to these different conditions, and so did the people who relied on them for food. As these first people became accustomed to life in the area, they stopped moving around to find food and water. They began building settlements and villages. While they still relied on hunting for food, they also began to grow crops such as corn, beans, and squash.

The different groups of early people in the Rocky Mountains developed into the Native American nations that we know today. The descendants of these first settlers still live in and around the region and are an important part of the history of the Rocky Mountains. These groups include the Apache, Crow, Ute, Shoshone, Nez Percé, Blackfeet, and Kootenai.

The Apache, also known as the Tinneh or Inde, lived in an area that stretched through Colorado, Arizona, New Mexico, Texas, and Mexico. The

Apache nourished themselves with wild plants, which made up over half of their diets. They lived in a type of dome-shaped shelter called the wickiup.

Apache woman

The Crow people's homelands are in the eastern part of the Rockies. The Crow are known for their impressive beadwork, which they made to decorate their clothing, horses, weapons, and more.

Crow beadwork

Ute man

The Ute, or Nuuchu, lived in what is now western Colorado and eastern Utah. The state of Utah is named after them. They used native plants like the yucca to make baskets, shoes, and even soap. They also tanned elk and deer skins. (Tanning is the process of turning animal skins into leather.)

Sacagawea

The Shoshone, or Newe, made their home in parts of modern-day Wyoming, Montana, Utah, and Idaho. Sacagawea was Shoshone. She helped the Lewis and Clark expedition succeed through her skill as a translator, her knowledge of parts of the land, and as a symbol of peace.

The traditional homeland of the Nez Percé, or Nimiipuu, is now Idaho and Montana. They became known for their skill at breeding horses and built up one of the largest horse herds in North America.

Nez Percé man

The Blackfeet called modern-day Montana and southern Alberta home. They were known as a powerful military force, dominating their area of the northern plains.

Blackfeet chief

Kootenai people

Kootenai (known as Ktunaxa in Canada) made their home in what is now southeastern British Columbia, northern Idaho, and northwestern Montana. They built bark and dugout canoes and engaged in communal fishing.

What's in a Name?

The name "Rocky Mountains" was first used by European explorers. The term was first mentioned by a French-speaking Canadian military officer in 1752. He described the mountain range as *montagnes de roche*, which means "rocky mountains" in French. When people who spoke English first heard the name in French, they simply translated the words. The name stuck. It was a very accurate way to describe the mountains to people who had never seen them.

However, the native people who had already been living in North America had different names for this magnificent mountain range. It is believed that the Cree first named the Rockies. They lived on the plains near the mountains and used the term *as-sin-wati* (written as ᐊᓯᐣᐘᑎ).

This translates to "seen across the plains." This name shows how easily the mountains could be seen from where they lived.

Cree people

CHAPTER 4
Early Explorers

Indigenous people had been living in the Rocky Mountain regions for thousands of years. However, the first Europeans did not arrive until the 1500s. The first European to record seeing the massive mountain range was Francisco Vázquez de Coronado, a Spanish conquistador (say: kon-KEE-sta-door). Conquistadors were soldiers who were sent to conquer new territory. Vásquez de Coronado led an expedition from 1540 to 1542 from present-day Mexico all the way to Kansas. He and his men were looking for the Seven Cities of Cíbola.

Francisco Vázquez de Coronado

They believed these cities, which were rumored to be filled with gold, might be somewhere in the southwestern area of North America.

Vásquez de Coronado didn't find the gold he was looking for, but he did encounter many groups of indigenous people. He and his men were also the first Europeans to see the Grand Canyon and the Colorado River. The Spanish continued to send conquistadors to what is now the American Southwest up until the 1700s.

Grand Canyon

Horses in North America

Native Americans are often shown riding horses in movies and in paintings. However, they did not have horses until the Spanish arrived in North America. Spanish conquistadors brought horses with them from Spain. Herds of wild horses came to be after a successful rebellion by the Pueblo nations, who rose up against Spanish colonial rulers in 1680 and drove them out of New Mexico. Hundreds of horses were left behind. They either passed into Native hands or escaped into the wild.

In the 1700s, French explorers started to enter the Rocky Mountain region. A pair of brothers, Louis-Joseph and François de La Vérendrye, may have been the first Europeans since Vásquez de Coronado's party to see the mountain range. On January 1, 1743, while the brothers were proceeding west, they spotted a range of huge mountains. They called them the "Shining Mountains."

Louis-Joseph and François de La Vérendrye

Then came Alexander Mackenzie, who was a fur trader and explorer. He was born in Scotland, but moved to Canada when he was a young man. Mackenzie was determined to find a route from Fort Chipewyan, in what is now modern-day Alberta, all the way to the Pacific Ocean. In 1789, he and a team of men set off on an expedition. However, they ended up at the Arctic Ocean. Convinced that he would still be able to find a route, he organized another expedition in 1793. When Mackenzie and his team were nearing the Rocky Mountains, his men begged him to turn around and head home. But Mackenzie was determined to reach his goal. This time he was successful. After crossing the Rockies, Mackenzie and his men

Alexander Mackenzie

eventually came to the Pacific Ocean along the coast of what is now called British Columbia. Mackenzie published a book about his expedition in 1801.

When President Thomas Jefferson heard that Alexander Mackenzie's expedition had reached the Pacific Ocean, he began making plans for a similar expedition for the United States. Jefferson wanted the team to explore and detail as much territory as possible. Jefferson chose Meriwether Lewis and William Clark to lead the expedition.

William Clark and Meriwether Lewis

In May 1804, they set off from Camp Wood in Illinois, but Lewis and Clark soon discovered that the Rocky Mountains were much higher and wider than they had expected. However, in August 1805, they crossed the Continental Divide at a place now called Lemhi Pass on the border of present-day Idaho and Montana.

When Lewis and Clark made it back to Illinois in 1806, the news of their expedition captured the attention of many Americans. More explorers became interested in finding routes to the western coast of North America. During the 1800s there were several expeditions to the region. In 1871, Ferdinand Hayden led a team that explored the area that is now Yellowstone National Park. Their reports of the waterfalls, hot springs, and geysers made people excited to search North America for more beautiful places. Mountaineer Hugh E. M. Stutfield and chemist J. Norman Collie were two Canadians who explored and reported on

David Thompson

the Canadian Rockies. Then, a man named David Thompson, who is often called the "Canadian Lewis and Clark," mapped over 1.9 million square miles in his lifetime. Much of it was in the Canadian section of the Rockies.

Explorers weren't the only people who were interested in heading west. Many Americans wanted to settle this territory and start new lives for themselves. During the mid- to late 1800s, the Oregon Trail was the route these people traveled along to make their way across North America. Over two thousand miles long, the trail ran from Independence, Missouri, to what is now northern Oregon. The trail crossed the Rocky Mountains in southern Wyoming at a place called the South Pass. Though many Americans saw the Oregon Trail as a positive, Native Americans saw it as a disaster. The travelers made their lives much more dangerous, as they introduced illness and were violent to tribes.

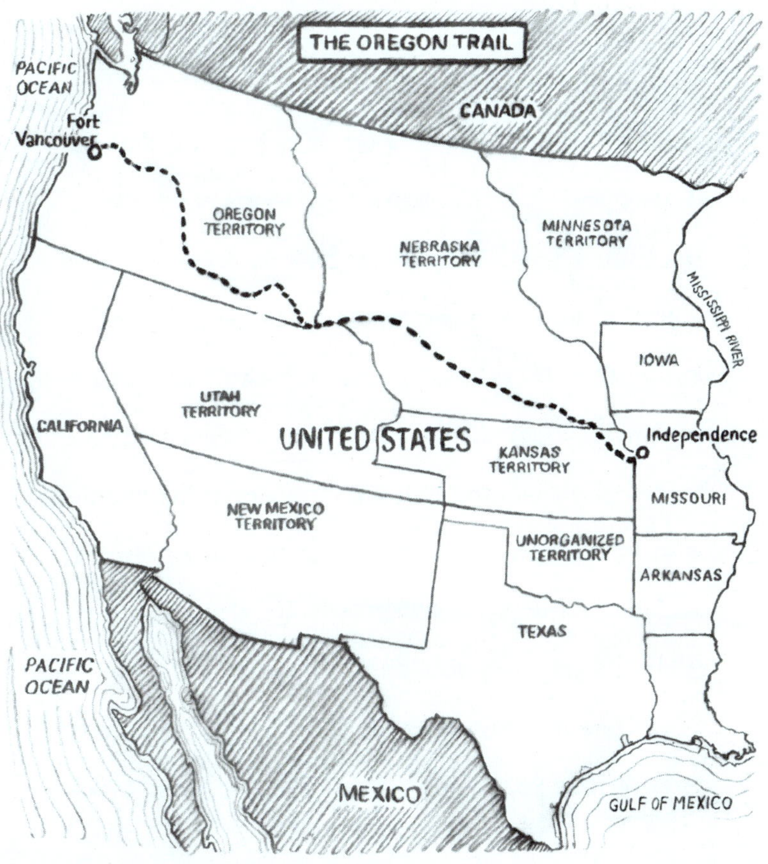

The Lewis and Clark Expedition

Starting in the 1600s, France explored and colonized areas of North America. Due to wars, the French were forced to give up much of this land. However, they did hold on to a large territory in the middle of the continent. In 1803, the United States bought this huge piece of territory from the French. It was west of the Mississippi River and called the Louisiana Purchase. The territory expanded the young nation from the Atlantic Ocean to the Rocky Mountains. President Thomas Jefferson was eager for this new part of the country to be explored and recorded. He wanted to learn more about the people who lived there, its waterways, natural resources, and possibilities for settlement. He also wanted to fill in the empty spaces on the maps at that time.

Jefferson chose Meriwether Lewis, who was twenty-nine years old, to lead a team of men. Lewis asked his friend William Clark to help him. Over the next two years they traveled about eight thousand miles with the help of Native American guides. One of these guides was George Drouillard. He was their main translator because he was fluent in English, French, and sign language.

Sacagawea guiding Lewis and Clark

It is believed that more than five hundred thousand people used the trail as they made their way west. But as more railroads were built and became the more popular way to travel, the Oregon Trail became quiet. However, ruts made by the wagon wheels can still be seen today.

Because of all the explorers and settlers who crossed the Rocky Mountains, by the end of the nineteenth century, the region was no longer a mystery.

CHAPTER 5
Life in the Mountains

The Rocky Mountains have areas that range from cold, rough mountain peaks and hot, dry deserts to cool, rainy forests and windy prairies. Because there are so many different kinds of environments, there is also a huge variety of plants and animals that live throughout the mountain range. In the northern areas, plants and animals must be able to survive harsh, snowy winters. Plants and animals in the southern regions, however, must be able to live in scorching temperatures and blazing sunshine. This range of plant and animal life in the Rockies is one of the main attractions of the mountain range. Millions of visitors make their way to the Rocky Mountains every year

to see these unique plants and animals in their native environments.

The Canadian and Northern Rockies are home to animals such as grizzly bears, mountain goats, great gray owls, and pikas, which are related to rabbits and are often called "rock rabbits." These animals

Pika

are able to deal with the jagged snowy peaks, dense forests, and freezing cold winters. Many of the animals, such as the bears and owls, hunt smaller prey, while the mountain goats and pikas depend on the grasses, moss, and lichens that grow in the northern areas of the Rockies. (Lichens are plantlike organisms that grow in moist areas, such as the bark on trees and where water runs down rocks.) Besides grasses, moss, and lichens, you can also find several species of pine trees, wildflowers, and shrubs in the Canadian and Northern Rockies. Just like the animals, the plants that live in this very northern region of the Rockies have adapted to living in cold temperatures for most of the year.

The Middle Rockies are home to some of the most well-known animals that live in the mountain range, including bison, moose, and gray wolves. You will also find coyotes, bighorn sheep, bald eagles, marmots (which are rodents that are related to prairie dogs), and garter snakes. These animals are able to deal with cold winters and hot summers. The predators feed on the huge variety of prey that live in the region, including elk, rabbits, and chipmunks. These often-hunted animals eat the trees, shrubs, and other plants that grow there, including ponderosa pine trees, Rocky Mountain juniper trees, Boulder raspberry shrubs, and needlegrass.

Gray wolf and Rocky Mountain juniper trees

Plants as Medicine

Many of the plants that grow in the Rocky Mountains were a source of food for the first native people. However, these people also relied on a variety of special plants as their sources of medicine. The indigenous people discovered that certain plants could be used to treat a range of ailments and illnesses. The plants were either made into tea or dried and ground into a powder that could be eaten or applied to their skin. Here are a few examples of plants they used:

- Sagebrush was used to prevent infection in wounds and treat headaches and colds.
- Bloodroot was used to treat sore throats, asthma, and fevers.
- Mesquite was used to treat irritated eyes and skin ailments.

- Purple coneflower helped relieve sores, swelling, and toothaches.
- Bitterroot was often used to control high blood pressure and diabetes.
- Agave was used to treat rashes, sunburn, and chapped lips.

Some of these plants are still used in medicines today to treat certain illnesses or conditions. However, only adults who work in medicine should be using these plants in their practice. These are *not* for kids to try at home, as that would be very dangerous.

Bloodroot

In the Southern Rockies, the temperatures increase and the amount of rainfall decreases compared to other sections of the mountains. Animals that live in this area must be able to cope with extreme heat and few water sources. Some of the animals of the Southern Rockies include mule deer, garter snakes, wild turkeys, prairie dogs, and greater short-horned lizards. The snakes, lizards, and some of the smaller mammals make their homes underground so that they can stay out of the sun and keep cool. In this part of the Rocky Mountains, you will find a variety of plants, from oak and pine trees to cacti and sagebrush.

Greater short-horned lizard

The southernmost region of the Rocky

Mountains is the Colorado Plateau. This area is not near a major city or even close to many homes, but it has some of the most spectacular sights in the world. The plants and animals in this area have adapted to survive in a dry region with cold winters and hot summer days that are followed by cool summer nights. Animals that live in this desert region include pronghorns (which look similar to antelope), red-tailed hawks, turkey vultures, desert cottontails, and rattlesnakes. Plants found here include bristlecone pine trees, Utah juniper trees, and a variety of cacti and wildflowers.

Pronghorn

Endangered Species

The Rocky Mountains are home to thousands of species of plants and animals. However, many species are endangered or have already gone extinct. An endangered species is any type of plant or animal that is in danger of disappearing forever because there are so few of their species left. If a species of plant or animal completely dies out, it becomes extinct.

Over the past hundred years, more and more people have moved into the area to live and work. People have used the land for farming, mining, logging, and tourism. And as more people have moved in, plants and animals have lost their homes. The lack of water, due to climate change, is also threatening the wildlife and plants. Some of the species that are threatened across the Rocky Mountains include the Canada lynx, the black-footed ferret, the Mexican gray wolf, the yellow-billed cuckoo, the greenback cutthroat trout, and the Pima pineapple cactus.

Canada lynx

However, people now realize it is important to protect all the plants and animals that live in this area of North America, and they are working to save the endangered species. All plants and animals play an important role in the ecosystem.

CHAPTER 6
Treasure Trove

The Rocky Mountains cover a huge area of North America. Because of that, they hold huge amounts of natural resources. These natural resources include common materials such as wood, grass, water, and rock, but also less common materials such as coal, oil, turquoise, and gold. The indigenous people of the Rocky Mountains have always made use of the natural resources around them. They used what they found in nature to survive and thrive. Rocks were transformed into tools and helped pound grain into flour. Animal skins were used for clothing and shoes. Sod and timber were used to build shelters. Turquoise, copper, and silver were mined for meaningful pieces of jewelry and decoration.

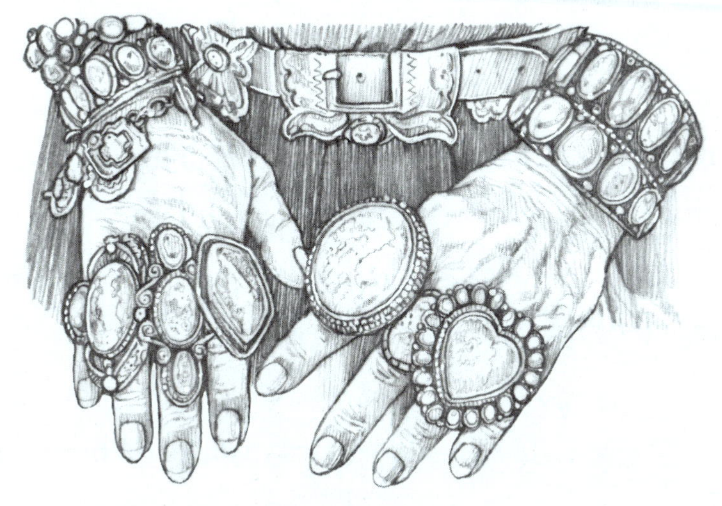

Turquoise jewelry

Vásquez de Coronado, the Spanish conquistador, didn't find gold during his exploration of the region. However, Spanish explorers who came to the territory after him did mine small amounts of valuable metals and minerals, including gold and silver. The explorers sent the metals and minerals back to Spain. These findings helped Spain become one of the wealthiest nations in the world at that time.

Once other European explorers and settlers arrived in the 1800s, the environment of the Rocky Mountains changed forever. The explorers and settlers discovered that the region was full of natural resources, and they did not wait to take much of these resources for themselves.

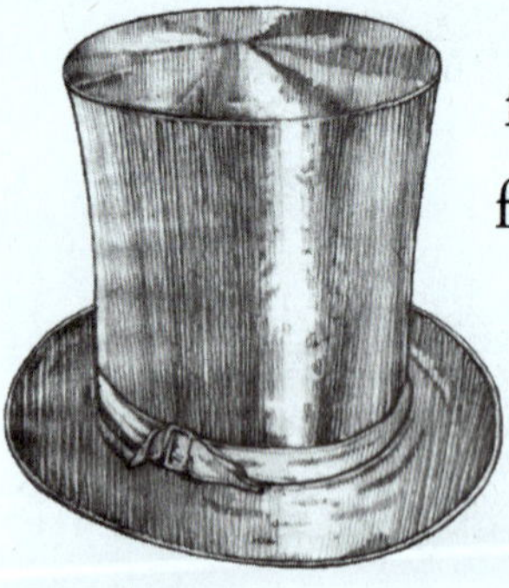

In the early 1800s, beaver fur was very valuable and used for making men's hats. Fur trappers came to the Rocky Mountains and almost wiped out the entire beaver population.

Beaver-fur hat

In 1858, prospectors found gold in what is now Colorado. (A prospector is a person who searches for precious metals and minerals.) When this news got out, tens of thousands of people rushed to the area. They panned for gold in the streams and rivers and dug for gold that might be deep in the ground.

While the prospectors were searching for the precious gold, they also found other natural resources, such as lead and zinc.

Going for Gold

In 1848, gold was discovered at Sutter's Mill in Northern California. As soon as the discovery was made public, thousands of people headed west to the area, hoping to strike it rich. This was the California Gold Rush of 1849. While many people did find gold in this gold rush, many did

Sutter's Mill

not, and they headed back east. On their way back through the Rockies, in what is now Colorado, some of these men discovered gold and another gold rush began.

In the first year, some 50,000 fortune hunters came to Colorado. The following year, gold was discovered in Idaho, attracting another 10,000 gold seekers. In 1862, gold was found in Montana, and by 1865 more than 120,000 people had arrived there hoping to be one of the lucky people who found gold. In 1861, Colorado alone produced 9,000 pounds of gold. By 1865, more than 78,000 pounds of gold had been produced.

While the gold rush was exciting for some, it was heartbreaking for others. Many Native Americans were killed by people who came to look for gold. There were 300,000 Native Americans in California before 1848. By 1870, their numbers were reduced to 30,000.

In the early 1860s, oil was discovered in the Rocky Mountains. Oil had become an important part of the economy at the time. At first it was used to lubricate machinery and to light lamps, and later, by the early twentieth century, it was also used to heat homes, manufacture goods, and build roads. Soon, oil wells were popping up across the Rocky Mountain landscape.

Sawmill

Around that time, lumber and sawmills were also established across the mountain range. Lumber is wood from trees that have been cut down. Millions of trees were cut down to supply this wood that was used to build homes, stores, factories, and railroads all throughout North America.

By the late 1800s, the number of people and new technologies made it easier for more and more natural resources to be taken from the Rocky Mountains. Because of these resources, the United States was able to make more goods and sell them to other countries. The resources helped many industries grow in the United States and helped the country become a wealthy nation.

After the US Civil War, the country's economy exploded. Coal production increased, and thousands of miles of railroad tracks were built. By the 1880s, the United States produced more steel and manufactured more goods than any other country in the world. The country was booming thanks in part to the natural resources of the Rocky Mountains. Canada experienced a similar boom in the late 1800s and early 1900s.

However, by the late 1800s, some people realized that it was harmful to the environment to continue to remove so many natural resources from the Rocky Mountain region. Since then, many organizations have been formed to help protect the region's public lands. These organizations work to preserve this incredible area of North America and make sure that it can be enjoyed by future generations.

CHAPTER 7
Welcome to the Rocky Mountains!

Some of the explorers who had documented the amazing landscapes in the Rocky Mountains believed that the area should be set aside for everyone to enjoy. These people believed that the United States government should take care of these important mountains rather than simply using the land for resources.

In March 1872, President Ulysses S. Grant signed an order to establish Yellowstone National Park, which covers parts of modern-day Wyoming, Montana, and Idaho. It was the very first national park to be created in the United States. The area was to be "set apart as a public park or pleasuring-ground for the benefit and enjoyment of the people." Many miners, loggers, and farmers were against creating the park. They wanted to continue using the area as a resource to make money. But by creating the park, no one would be allowed to own the land, and thus strip it of its natural resources or build on it. It would be preserved and protected, instead of settled on and developed.

Ulysses S. Grant

During January 1915, President Woodrow Wilson signed the Rocky Mountain National Park Act, creating Rocky Mountain National Park in Colorado. Today, there are five national parks across the massive Rocky Mountain region of the United States: Yellowstone, Rocky Mountain, Glacier (established in 1910 in Montana), Grand Teton (established in 1929 in Wyoming), and Great Sand Dunes (established in 1932 in Colorado).

Great Sand Dunes

In the United States, the Rocky Mountains are also home to six national monuments, five national historic sites, and one national battlefield. The national monuments include the Canyons of the Ancients National Monument in Colorado, which has amazing archaeological sites, and Florissant Fossil Beds, also in Colorado, which has some of the world's most diverse insect and animal fossils.

Florissant Fossil Beds

Banff National Park

Canada established its first national park, Banff National Park in the province of Alberta, in 1885. Just as the United States government had done with Yellowstone, the Canadian government wanted to protect this unique area. Since then,

Canada has established four other national parks in the Rocky Mountain area: Jasper, Kootenay, Yoho, and Waterton Lakes. In 1984, the Canadian Rocky Mountain Parks were named a World Heritage site by a special agency at the United Nations. (The United Nations, known as the UN, works to improve people's lives around the world in lots of ways.) A World Heritage site is chosen because it has "outstanding universal value." Being designated a World Heritage site shows the importance of keeping these kinds of areas safe and undeveloped so that they can be enjoyed by visitors now and into the future.

Every year, millions of people travel from around the world to visit the big national parks in the Rocky Mountains. They come throughout the year to see the breathtaking landscapes and take photos of the unique plants and animals, as well as camp, hike, fish, boat, and lots of other activities. In Yellowstone, you can snap pictures of the spouting geysers and bubbling hot springs. In Banff, you can canoe on the beautiful turquoise waters of Lake Louise. You can explore the 355 miles of hiking trails in Rocky Mountain National Park. And you can go snowshoeing through forests at Yoho National Park.

In Canada, there are also provincial parks in addition to the national parks. These are maintained by the provinces of Canada. Mount

Assiniboine and Hamber Parks are located in the province of British Columbia. These parks are in deep wilderness areas, and no roads run through them. The only way visitors can explore the parks is by hiking trail, boat, or helicopter.

There is so much to see and do if you visit the Rocky Mountains. However, because of the incredible landscapes and wildlife, there are also things to be aware of if you visit. For instance, if you do go hiking, make sure you always stay on the designated trails, as steep cliffs, bubbling hot springs, and rushing streams can be dangerous.

While you may want to get as close as you can to a grazing bison, berry-eating bear, or busy beaver, it's important to keep your distance. When you visit a park in the Rocky Mountains, you need to remember that the place is home to these animals and that you need to be respectful. These creatures are wild, and they won't like it if you try to get too close.

Walking on Ice and Air

Visitors from all over the world travel to the Columbia Icefield in Canada, which is the largest ice field in North America's Rocky Mountains.

If you visit the Columbia Icefield, you can hike on the ice. But there is something else very exciting to do there—take a stroll on the Skywalk. The Columbia Icefield Skywalk is a glass platform that is suspended 918 feet above the rocks below. It's almost like you're walking on air. From the Skywalk, you get a bird's-eye view of the ice field, the mountains, the waterfalls, and the wildlife. From up high, you can get a real sense of how massive the Rocky Mountains are.

Columbia Icefield Skywalk

CHAPTER 8
Preserve and Protect

The Rocky Mountains are millions of years old. They run for more than three thousand miles down the western side of North America. They cover more than three hundred thousand square miles. (That's a third larger than the entire country of France.) Still, much of the mountain range is remote and uninhabited. Given these facts, it might seem like this ancient and massive mountain range would have no problem surviving well into the future. However, just because they are very old and take up a lot of space doesn't mean that the mountains will stay the way they are forever.

Many areas of the Rocky Mountains have become very popular places for people to live and take vacations. In 1900, the population of Denver, Colorado, was around 134,000. One hundred years later, the population had grown to about 557,000. That's a four-fold increase! Many towns and cities throughout the Rocky Mountains have experienced this kind of growth. People are attracted to the beautiful scenery, the outdoor lifestyle, and the job opportunities.

If more people move to this area of the continent, however, more space and resources will be needed to provide them with energy, water, food, and housing. All of this puts a strain on the environment. Building new houses often means that people and wildlife come into contact with each other, which can be dangerous for humans and harmful to animals. Drilling for oil and cutting down trees destroys the animals' habitats. If their homes are destroyed, they don't have anywhere to go. More people leads to more cars and trucks, which create pollution. This is bad for people, animals, and plants.

All these factors have an impact on how quickly and severely the climate is changing. Earth's climate has always gone through changes, and there have been many periods of warming and cooling in Earth's history. But over the past century or so, human activity has caused the climate to warm faster and more extremely. The harmful gases that are released by the increased pollution have caused Earth's temperature to rise every year. A warmer planet is a threat to life in the Rocky Mountains and all around the world.

One of the biggest threats to the Rocky Mountains is something made worse by climate change: wildfires. In the past few years, wildfires have caused destruction to the wild, open spaces and the towns across the Rocky Mountains. Very hot summers and very dry winters caused by climate change mean that the smallest spark from a campfire or power line can set a horrible wildfire in motion. In the summer of 2024, wildfires in British Columbia and Alberta meant that fifteen thousand visitors to Jasper National Park had to be evacuated to get out of the fire's fast path.

In the fall of 2020, Colorado experienced two of the largest wildfires in the state's history. These fires were mainly on the land surrounding Rocky Mountain National Park, but about thirty thousand acres inside the park were destroyed by the fire. (That's an area about the size of twenty-three thousand football fields.)

Landslides are another threat to the Rocky Mountains. A landslide occurs when a mass of rock, dirt, or debris moves down a slope. This can happen suddenly or over a period of time, and landslides can move slowly or very quickly. Some landslides can move faster than a person can run. They usually occur where trees have been removed from a slope, either due to logging, the need for grazing land for animals, or wildfires. There are no tree roots to absorb the water from rain or snow, so the heavy soil begins to shift and slide. In June 2024, a landslide wiped out a large section of a two-lane highway in Wyoming.

Landslide

It might seem that climate change and the effect that it has on our planet and the Rocky Mountains can't be stopped. The US and Canadian governments realize that it's important to protect this magnificent mountain range and its resources, along with the plants and animals that live there. Various laws have been passed to help achieve this goal. Organizations and charities have been set up to raise money to work to protect and preserve the land and the wildlife across the Rocky Mountain region.

There are things we can all do to make sure that we preserve and protect this incredible mountain range for future generations to enjoy. If you do get a chance to visit the Rocky Mountains, make sure you follow the "Leave No Trace" policy. This policy was created to minimize the impact of human activities on the natural world. Some

of the policy's rules require visitors to dispose of waste properly, respect wildlife, be considerate to other visitors, leave what you find, stay on designated paths and trails, and minimize the impact of campfires.

Even if you aren't planning a visit to the Rocky Mountains, there are still things you can do to reduce your "footprint" on the natural world. Here are some suggestions: Encourage your family to drive a more fuel-efficient or an electric car, ride your bike instead of riding in a car whenever you can, keep the temperature in the house lower in the winter and warmer in the summer, turn off lights when you're not using them and when you leave a room, and reuse and recycle whatever you

can. All these things help reduce the amount of energy and resources you use, which helps reduce the effects of climate change.

The mighty Rocky Mountains have been around for millions of years, and hopefully they will be around for millions more. But we all need to do our part to make sure that happens.

Can a River Dry Up?

The Colorado River is one of the main rivers in the southwestern United States. It is 1,450 miles long and supplies water for almost forty million people in Colorado, New Mexico, Utah, Wyoming, Arizona, California, and Nevada, and two Mexican states.

The Colorado River

But the Colorado River is drying up because of overuse and climate change.

In the past fifty years, more and more people have been moving to the American Southwest in search of an outdoor lifestyle and warmer temperatures. Because of this, more water has been needed for homes, farms, and businesses, as well as golf courses, parks, and other recreational areas. This region of the country has also experienced a severe drought for the past twenty years, so the water in the river is not being replenished by rainfall or melting snow. The Colorado River, which was once wild and roaring, is now just a muddy trickle in some spots.

The United States government is now working with the southwestern states, as well as groups of indigenous people, affected by the lack of water. They are asking the people of these areas to cut down on their use of water.

Timeline of the Rocky Mountains

mya = million years ago

c. 300 mya	Ancestral Rocky Mountains begin to form
c. 10 mya	Present-day Rocky Mountains form
c. 14,000 years ago	Settlers who are thought to have come from Asia arrive in the Rocky Mountain region
c. 1190s	Cliff dwellings at Mesa Verde (in modern-day Colorado) are built
1540–1542	Francisco Vásquez de Coronado explores the southwestern Rocky Mountain region
1743	French explorers Louis-Joseph and François de La Vérendrye report seeing the Rocky Mountains
1793	Alexander Mackenzie leads an expedition in the Canadian Rockies
1805	Lewis and Clark cross the Continental Divide
1872	Yellowstone National Park is established
1907	Jasper National Park is established by the Canadian government
1913–1920	Fall River Road, first road to cross the Rockies, is built in Colorado
1931	Rocky Mountain Conservancy is founded
2000	Megadrought begins in the southwestern region of the Rocky Mountains
2024	Wildfires burn in British Columbia and Alberta

Timeline of the World

500 mya	Plants begin to flourish on land
65 mya	Dinosaurs die out on Earth
c. 200,000 BCE	*Homo sapiens* (modern humans) first appear
c. 11,500 BCE	The last ice age ends
c. 3150 BCE	Start of ancient Egyptian civilization
c. 27 BCE	Start of the ancient Roman Empire
1066 CE	The Norman Conquest of England
1492	Christopher Columbus sails to the New World
1620	Pilgrims sail from England to North America on the *Mayflower*
1803	The Louisiana Purchase doubles the size of the United States
1861–1865	The US Civil War is fought
1920	The Nineteenth Amendment is ratified, giving women in the United States the right to vote
1939–1945	World War II is fought
1963	Martin Luther King Jr. gives his "I Have a Dream" speech
1994	Nelson Mandela is elected president of South Africa
2024	Hurricane Helene hits Florida, North Carolina, Virginia, and Georgia, among other states

Bibliography

***Books for young readers**

*Aloian, Molly. ***The Rocky Mountains***. Mountains Around the World. New York: Crabtree Publishing, 2012.

*Bauer, Marion Dane. ***The Rocky Mountains***. Wonders of America. New York: Simon Spotlight, 2006.

Cannings, Richard. ***The Rockies: A Natural History***. Vancouver, Canada: Greystone Books, 2005.

Elias, Scott A. ***Rocky Mountains***. Washington, DC: Smithsonian Institution Press, 2002.

Ferguson, Gary. ***The Great Divide: A Biography of the Rocky Mountains***. Woodstock, VT: The Countryman Press, 2004.

Frémont, John Charles. ***Narrative of the Exploring Expedition to the Rocky Mountains***. Charleston, SC: Arcadia Publishing, 2018.

Hecox, Walter E. "Rockies Region Natural Resources: The Foundation for Economy and Quality of Life—Then, Now, Tomorrow." Headwaters Economics. May 7, 2018. https://headwaterseconomics.org/public-lands/papl-hecox/.

"Horses in North America: A Comeback Story." ***Nature***. February 25, 2022. https://www.pbs.org/wnet/nature/blog/american-horses-horses-in-north-america-a-comeback-story/.

*Lynch, Wayne. ***Rocky Mountains***. Our Wide World. Minnetonka, MN: NorthWord, 2006.

McPhee, John. ***Rising From the Plains***. New York: Farrar Straus and Giroux, 1986.

Newby, Rick (editor). ***The Rocky Mountain Region***. The Greenwood Encyclopedia of American Regional Cultures. Westport, CT: Greenwood Press, 2004.

"Rocky Mountains." ***Britannica***. Last updated February 27, 2025. https://www.britannica.com/place/Rocky-Mountains.

"Rocky Mountains." ***WorldAtlas***. https://www.worldatlas.com/mountains/rocky-mountains.html.

Websites

nps.gov

parks.canada.ca

WHOHQ

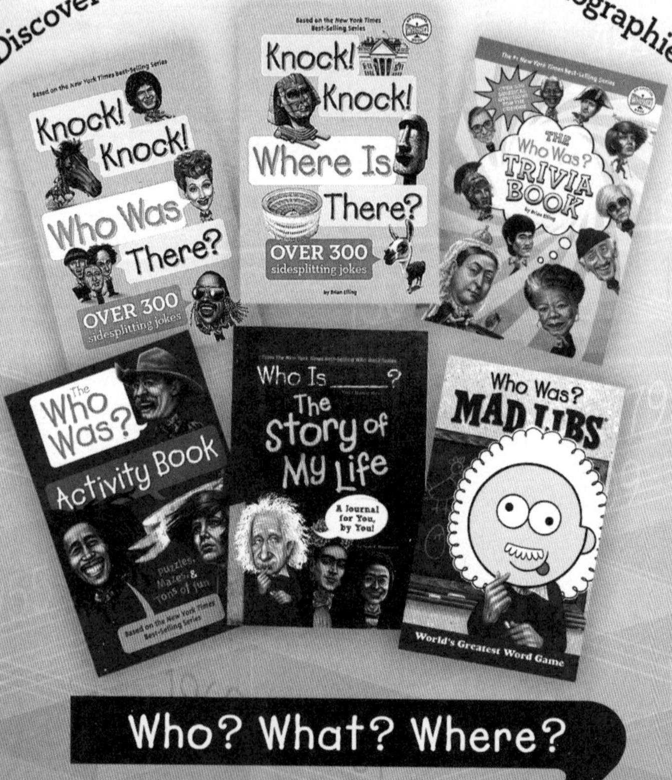